The North West

Reasor and sea

The North West includes the counties of Cumbria, Lancashire, Cheshire, Greater Manchester and Merseyside, and is increasingly becoming well known for the wide variety and quality of its produce.

The scenery influences the food; from lush meadows to dramatic lakes and mountains, and vibrant cities. The range of produce is equally diverse. A wonderful selection of red meats, poultry, smoked meats and fish, traditional bacon, hams and sausages, real ales and ciders, fresh vegetables, salads, herbs, seasonal soft fruits and apples, speciality cheeses, yoghurts, and ice cream, bakery and confectionery, rich traditional puddings and much, much more.

Local food has not travelled so far and is likely to be fresher

Packaging is usually minimal, so it is better for the environment

Food in season is fresher and cheaper

You can trace where the food has come from and be more confident about its quality and traceability

You can help the local economy and keep jobs in the region

For more information go to www.nwfinefood.co.uk

A guide to Seasonal Produce

Spring

MARCH

Cabbage
Carrots
Cauliflower
Early Rhubarb
Leeks
Onions
Parsley
Potatoes
Protected Spinach
Purple Sprouting
Broccoli
Radishes
Swede
Spring Greens
Winter Root Crops

APRIL

Carrots
Cauliflower
Early Rhubarb
Leeks
New Potatoes
Onions
Parsley
Potatoes
Protected Spinach
Purple Sprouting
Broccoli
Radishes
Spring Greens
Spring Onion
Watercress

MAY

Asparagus
Beetroot
Broad Beans
Kale
Leeks
Lettuce
Mushrooms
New Potatoes
Onions
Radishes
Rhubarb
Spring Greens
Spring Lamb
Spring Onions
Watercress

Summer

JUNE

Asparagus
Beetroot
Broad Beans
Cabbage
Carrots
Courgettes
Gooseberries
Lettuce
New Potatoes
Peas
Rhubarb
Salad Leaves
Strawberries
Watercress

JULY

Beetroot
Blackcurrants
Broad Beans
Carrots
Cherries
Courgettes
Cucumber
French Beans
Gooseberries
Lettuce
Loganberries
Potatoes
Peas
Radishes
Raspberries
Rhubarb
Redcurrants

AUGUST

Aubergines
Beetroot
Broad Beans
Broccoli
Carrots
Celery
Cherries
Chillies
Courgettes
Cucumber
Fennel
French Beans
Garlic
Gooseberries
Lettuce
Onions
Peas

Autumn

SEPTEMBER

Apples
Aubergines
Beetroot
Bilberries
Blackberries
Blueberries
Brussel Sprouts
Cabbage (Autumn)
Celery
Damsons
Leeks
Marrows
Plums
Potatoes (Main Crop)
Sloes
Sweetcorn

OCTOBER

Beetroot
Brussel Sprouts
Cabbage
Celeriac
Celery
Chestnuts
Cobnuts
Crab Apples
Fennel
Field Mushrooms
Hazelnuts
Jerusalem Artichokes
Main Crop Potatoes
Marrow
Partridge
Pheasant
Pigeon
Quince
Rabbit
Spinach
Squash
Turnip
Venison
Watercress

NOVEMBER

Apples
Aubergines
Beetroot
Bilberries
Blackberries
Blueberries
Brussel Sprouts
Cabbage
Celery
Cobnuts
Damsons
Grouse
Hare
Leeks
Marrows
Partridge
Pheasant
Pigeon
Plums
Potatoes
Rabbit
Sloes
Sweetcorn
Venison
Wild Duck

Many experts believe that autumn lamb has more flavour and is more succulent than spring lamb.

Winter

DECEMBER

Apples
Beetroot
Broccoli
Brussel Sprouts
Cabbage (Winter)
Carrots
Cauliflower
Celeriac
Celery (White Winter)
Grouse
Jerusalem Artichokes
Leeks
Onions
Parsnips
Partridge
Pears
Pheasant
Potatoes
Pumpkin
Rabbit
Spinach
Swede
Turnip
Venison

JANUARY

Apples
Beetroot
Broccoli (Purple Sprouting)
Brussels sprouts
Cabbage (Winter)
Carrots
Cauliflower
Celeriac
Celery
Goose
Grouse
Jerusalem Artichokes
Leeks
Onions
Parsnips
Pears
Pheasant
Potatoes
Pumpkin
Rabbit
Spinach
Swede
Turnip
Venison

FEBRUARY

Apples
Brussel Sprouts
Carrots
Celeriac
Chard
Forced Rhubarb
Jerusalem Artichokes
Leeks
Mussels
Onions
Pears
Potatoes
Protected Spinach
Purple Sprouting Broccoli
Swede
Turnip

Spring

MARCH, APRIL, MAY

Cullen Skink

Twice Baked Lancashire Cheese Soufflé

Asparagus with Cumbrian Air Dried Ham

Wine Coated Spring Greens

Potato Frittata

Beef Stir Fry

Pasta with Spicy Purple Sprouting Broccoli

Warm Strawberry, Spring Rhubarb and Ginger Compote

Seasonal Produce:

Carrots, Cauliflower, Early Rhubarb, Leeks, Onions, Parsley, New Potatoes, Protected Spinach, Purple Sprouting Broccoli, Radishes, Swede, Spring Greens, Winter Root Crops, Spring Onion, Watercress, Beetroot, Broad Beans, Kale, Leeks, Lettuce, Mushrooms, Spring Lamb, Cabbage.

Cullen Skink (Smoked haddock and potato broth)

SERVES 2 AS A COMPLETE MEAL OR 4 FOR A STARTER

This is a delicious meal using vegetables grown in the North West and haddock smoked on the Lancashire coast. Really warming and comforting and quite easy to make.

INGREDIENTS:
50g butter / 125g leeks, thinly sliced / 1 garlic clove, crushed
125g onions, finely diced / 40g plain flour
250g small potatoes, peeled and cubed / 1 litre water
1 fish stock cube / 250g smoked undyed haddock, skinned, boned and cut into 2cm chunks / 45ml double cream
1 tbsp fresh chopped chives
Sea salt and fresh black pepper to taste

METHOD
1. Put the butter, leeks, garlic and onions into a heavy bottomed pan and on a low heat fry gently for 10 minutes without colouring.
2. Add the flour and mix very well
3. Make the stock up with the water, add a ladle at a time of the stock to the vegetable mixture over a low heat, stirring continuously with a wooden spoon until you have a smooth slightly thickened mix.
4. Add the potatoes and bring to the boil, simmer this gently for 20 minutes or until the potatoes are cooked.
5. Add the haddock and stir in gently, season to taste.
6. Simmer for another 5 minutes.
7. Add the cream and ladle into warm bowls and garnish with chopped chives.

Twice Baked Lancashire Cheese Soufflé

SERVES 6
Make these the day before you want to serve them so no last minute panics. Serve them with a green salad or purple sprouting broccoli.

INGREDIENTS:
225ml milk / 1 small onion chopped / 1 bay leaf
25g butter plus a little extra to grease the ramekin dishes
25g flour / 1/2 tsp mustard / 3 large eggs separated
225g tasty Lancashire cheese grated / Salt and pepper to taste

METHOD
1. Preheat the oven to 180C. Grease 6 ramekin dishes with the extra butter.
2. Put milk, onion and bay leaf in a saucepan, bring to the boil and then leave for 10 minutes before straining.
3. Melt the butter in a pan and stir in the flour, remove from the heat then add the mustard.
4. Gradually add the milk stirring all the time until the mixture is smooth, you can use a whisk.
5. Return to the heat and bring to the boil stirring well. Remove from the heat, add 200g of the cheese and the egg yolks and stir in well.
6. Season to taste.
7. Whisk the egg whites until very stiff and gently fold into the cheese mixture, divide between the 6 dishes.
8. Place the dishes in a roasting tin and pour boiling water in to half way up the sides of the dishes, place in the oven. Cook for 20 minutes until pale gold and set.
9. Cool and chill until needed.

TO FINISH
Preheat the oven to 200°C. Top the soufflés with the remaining cheese and bake for 20 minutes until risen and golden. Serve immediately.

Baked Asparagus with Air Dried Ham

SERVES 4 AS A STARTER OR LIGHT SUPPER

Local asparagus is only available for a short time; make the most of it in this recipe. Thinner asparagus is good for this.

INGREDIENTS:

Approximately 36 spears of fresh asparagus, woody ends trimmed off
100g Cumbrian air dried ham, thinly sliced and cut into 12 pieces.
A little olive oil for drizzling / Salt and freshly ground pepper to taste.

METHOD

1. Preheat oven to 200°C.
2. Take 3 spears of asparagus and wrap one piece of air dried ham around spears to hold them tightly.

3. Continue to do similar with all asparagus and ham.
4. Place bundles on a greased oven proof dish.
5. Drizzle with a little olive oil.
6. Bake in a pre-heated oven for 15 minutes or until asparagus is just tender and ham is crispy.
7. Serve 3 bundles per portion as a starter drizzled with a little more olive oil and seasoned to taste.

You can add a little tasty Lancashire cheese crumbled on the top if you wish.

Wine Glazed Spring Greens

SERVES 4

Spring greens are full of vitamins and minerals; they have a lovely sweet taste. Remove the tough outer leaves and the bottom of the stalk, wash the rest well and shred finely. This goes well with a roast and gives a modern twist to a traditional vegetable.

INGREDIENTS:

1 tbsp olive oil / 25g butter
50g dry cure smoked streaky bacon, rind removed and chopped
1 small onion, roughly chopped / 150ml dry white wine
1 garlic clove, crushed / 450g local spring greens, shredded
Salt and ground black pepper

METHOD

1. In a wok or large frying pan heat the oil and butter and add the bacon and onion and garlic. Fry for about 4 minutes until the onion is beginning to soften and the bacon is starting to brown slightly.

2. Add the wine and cook on high to reduce the liquid for about 2 minutes.
3. Lower the heat and add the spring greens and seasoning, mix well.
4. Cook over a gentle heat for about 3 minutes until the greens are tender. Serve immediately.

Potato Frittata

SERVES 2

This is based on an Italian recipe but it uses very traditional ingredients. It can be eaten hot straight from the pan or cooled and cut into wedges for lunch or picnics. This recipe can have cooked red, green and yellow peppers added, courgettes, onion, mushrooms, bacon, or peas. The choice is yours, all of them or just one or two added before the egg, the result will be delicious. This is an ideal way to use vegetables in season.

INGREDIENTS:

4 tbsp olive oil / Small onion sliced finely
2 medium potatoes, cooked and sliced / 4 free range eggs
4 tbsp water / Salt and pepper / 1 tbsp fresh parsley chopped

METHOD

1. Heat the oil in a 20cm frying pan and add the onion, cook for 3 minutes.
2. Pre heat the grill.
3. Add the potatoes and cook until they are beginning to brown, turn and cook the other side.

4. Beat the eggs, water and salt and pepper together and pour over the potatoes. Stir to spread evenly over.
5. When the eggs begin to set turn the heat down, be careful not to burn the base.
6. Put the pan under the grill to finish, you will find the eggs will go light brown and puff up slightly.
7. When the frittata is just set, slide out of the pan onto a large plate and serve.

Sweet and Sour Beef and Vegetables

SERVES 4

Try making your own sweet and sour rather than going to the takeaway. It is much better for you because you can cut down the fat and you know exactly what is in the dish. Many of the ingredients will already be in your cupboard. The trick with stir fries is to do all the preparation in advance and then it is really quick to cook. Serve this with noodles or boiled rice that you have stirred 100g of cooked frozen peas into.

INGREDIENTS:

4 tbsp tomato sauce / 2 tbsp tomato puree
4 tbsp sweet chilli sauce (optional) / 1 tbsp malt vinegar
2 tsp cornflour / 227g can of pineapple chunks in natural juice, drained but juice reserved / 3 tbsp sunflower oil
2 carrots peeled and cut into matchsticks or thin slices
1 onion roughly chopped / 1 clove of garlic
1 red pepper cut into strips / 1 green pepper cut into strips
5 spring onions sliced / 400g beef, rump, topside or sirloin is ideal, cut into thin strips / Salt and pepper to taste

METHOD

1. Place the tomato sauce, puree, chilli sauce and vinegar into a small pan.
2. Mix the cornflour with a little juice and then add to the pan with the rest of the juice.
3. Bring all the sauce ingredients to the boil stirring all the time and simmer for a couple of minutes. You should have a glossy slightly thickened sauce. Keep warm.
4. Heat 2 tbsp of the oil in a large pan or wok.
5. Stir in the carrots, onion and garlic, cook for 4 minutes.
6. Add the peppers and spring onions and cook for 3 minutes, add the drained pineapple.
7. Remove all the vegetables from the pan and keep warm.
8. Add the remaining tbsp of oil to the pan and heat. When it is hot stir in the meat, keep the heat high and cook the meat until it is browned this will only take a couple of minutes.

8\. Return the vegetables to the pan and mix, season to taste.

9\. Turn out onto a warmed serving dish and top with the sauce.

Pasta with Spicy Purple Sprouting Broccoli

SERVES 4

Purple sprouting broccoli has a short season in the spring but it is becoming widely available during this time. It has a lovely sweet flavour, but don't over cook it. It is great served with a little butter and picked up with your fingers, children love it. In this dish the anchovies will cook down and just add to the flavour so don't tell anyone they are in if you feel it may put them off! Be careful with the chilli, remove the seeds under running water and don't touch your eyes.

INGREDIENTS:

500g purple sprouting broccoli / 4 tbsp olive oil
1 medium red fresh chilli, seeds removed, and finely chopped
2 cloves garlic, peeled and chopped
1 small tin of anchovy fillets in olive oil, drained and chopped
300g good quality pasta, shells or similar / 75g tasty cheese grated
Pepper to taste

METHOD

1. Trim the broccoli to remove the woody ends of stalks and cut into 2 cm lengths, wash well.
2. Heat the oil in a pan and add the chilli, garlic and anchovies, cook for a minute then add the broccoli, stir and cook gently.

3. Meanwhile cook the pasta in a large pan of boiling salted water according to the directions on the packet.
4. Add a couple of tablespoons of the pasta water to the broccoli and cook for a few minutes more.
5. Stir the cheese into the broccoli and season to taste with pepper.
6. Drain the pasta and mix in the broccoli, serve immediately.

Warm Strawberry, Spring Rhubarb and Ginger Compote

SERVES 4

There is a time in May when you can buy the young rhubarb and the first of the forced strawberries on the farmers markets; this is the time to make this. It is the most glorious pink colour with a rich juice. Serve it with cream, the best custard or ice cream.

INGREDIENTS:

500g rhubarb / 50g caster sugar
50g stem ginger diced / 250g strawberries

METHOD

1. Wash and trim the rhubarb and cut into 2.5cm lengths.
2. Cook with the sugar and ginger and 3 tbsp water in a stainless steel pan with a lid until beginning to soften.
3. Stir in the strawberries, halved if necessary, remove from the heat.
4. Serve whilst still warm although this tastes good cold.

Summer

JUNE, JULY, AUGUST

Tomato Tart

Courgette, Mushroom and Tomato Gratin

Tabouleh

Minted Chicken Kebabs

Beef Burgers with Barbeque Sauce

Salmon Parcels

Cheese and Spring Onion

Summer Berry and Pancake Gateaux with Chantilly Cream

Seasonal Produce:

Carrots, Asparagus, Aubergines, Beans, Runner and Dwarf, Broad Beans, Broccoli, Cabbage, Cauliflower, Courgette, Cucumber, Fennel, Garlic, Lettuce, Mushrooms, Onions, Peas, Potatoes, Radishes, Rhubarb, Sweetcorn, Tomatoes, Watercress, Blackcurrants, Cherries, Gooseberries, Loganberries, Raspberries, Redcurrants, Strawberries.

Tomato Tart

SERVES 6

Tomatoes are especially delicious when they are in season and particularly good if they have not been picked too soon. Merseyside and Greater Manchester both have commercial growers who have fantastic tomatoes. This recipe brings out their excellent flavour and makes a starter to a meal or is great for a quick lunch. Top with cheese if you want to make a more substantial meal, a slice of goat's cheese goes particularly well.

INGREDIENTS:

350g puff pastry / 3 tbsp tomato chutney / 2 tsp pesto
8 ripe, medium-sized tomatoes / Salt and freshly ground pepper
1 tsp sugar - to taste / 1/2 tsp fresh thyme leaves / 1 tbsp olive oil

METHOD

1. Preheat the oven to 220C.
2. Roll out the pastry thinly to a 30cm square. Cut into 6 to make 10cm x 10cm squares. If using a ready rolled pastry each sheet will cut into 4.
3. Mark a line with a knife without cutting all the way through round the edge of the pastry.
4. Mix the chutney with the pesto.

5. Place the pastry squares on a baking sheet. Spread 1 tsp of the tomato mixture over each square up to the line leaving a border all the way around the edges.
6. Slice the tomatoes as thinly as you can.
7. Arrange the tomato rings on the pastry and season with salt, pepper and a little sugar to taste.
8. Scatter over the thyme and drizzle over the olive oil.
9. Bake in the oven for 12-15 minutes until golden brown and risen. Serve warm.

Courgette, Mushroom and Tomato Gratin

SERVES 4

There is a time late summer when courgettes are very cheap and tomatoes are plentiful, try this dish then. Serve it as a complete meal with jacket potatoes. Alternatively you can serve it as a vegetable with steak, chops or chicken.

INGREDIENTS:

50g butter / 4 medium courgettes sliced
1 medium onion finely chopped / 2 cloves garlic peeled and chopped
250g mushrooms sliced / 350g tomatoes roughly chopped
250g half fat crème fraiche / 1/2 tsp thyme leaves
1 tbsp parsley roughly chopped / 50g fresh breadcrumbs
50g grated tasty Lancashire Cheese

METHOD

1. Preheat the oven to 200C
2. Heat half the butter in a large pan and quickly fry the courgettes and onion until beginning to brown. Remove into an oven proof, shallow casserole dish.
3. Heat the rest of the butter and add the garlic and mushrooms, cook for 4 minutes.
4. Now add the tomatoes and cook for 4 minutes, stir in the thyme, parsley and the cream.
5. Bring to the boil and check the seasonings, add salt and pepper to taste.
6. Stir in the courgettes and then return to the casserole dish.
7. Mix together the breadcrumbs and cheese and sprinkle over the top of the courgette mixture.
8. Cook in the oven for 20 - 30 minutes or until the topping is golden. Serve at once.

Tabouleh

SERVES 4

This is really economical to make but has a very fresh taste and a crunchy texture. It will keep in the fridge for a couple of days and is served as a salad, great with burgers or kebabs. You can buy bulgar wheat in a health food store very cheaply. If you wish you can use cous cous instead, but follow the directions on the packet.

INGREDIENTS:

100g bulgar wheat (sometimes called cracked wheat)
1 large tomato diced / 4 spring onions sliced finely
1 cucumber seeded and finely diced / Handful of fresh mint chopped
Handful of fresh parsley chopped
Salt and freshly ground pepper to taste / 3 tbsp Olive oil
3 tbsp lemon juice

METHOD

1. Soak the wheat in cold water for 2 hours or as directed on the packet.
2. Drain well in a sieve and press out any excess water.

3. Mix all the ingredients together in a large bowl.
4. Cover and chill before serving.

Minted Chicken Kebabs

SERVES 4

This is an ideal BBQ dish, use a good quality, locally reared, free range chicken and you can be sure this is going to be good for you. Marinate the chicken for at least 3 hours. If you want to make these more economical use boneless, skinless chicken thighs, you will need 6-8 depending on size. Serve with tabouleh or jacket potatoes and a green salad.

INGREDIENTS:

75ml natural yoghurt / 1 clove of garlic crushed
5 sprigs fresh mint, chopped / 2 tsp white wine vinegar
Salt, freshly ground pepper / 3 chicken breasts each cut into 12
2 yellow peppers each cut into 8 / 2 red onions, each cut into 3
Olive oil for brushing

Kebab sticks or skewers (If you use wooden sticks soak them in water before use)

METHOD

1. Mix the yoghurt, garlic, mint, wine vinegar and seasoning.
2. Pour over the chicken chunks. Mix well, cover and chill.
3. Allow to marinade for 3-4 hours.
4. To make up the skewers, thread alternating pieces of chicken, peppers and onion.
4. Brush with olive oil
5. Grill for 15-20 minutes, turning during cooking or bake in a hot oven 200C for 20 minutes until nicely browned.

Beef Burgers with Barbeque Sauce

SERVES 4

These are easy to make and much better than buying ready made. You can make these to your taste and that way you know exactly what goes in them. The secret is to use good quality, lean minced steak not the cheapest you can find, but there will be no waste. The sauce can be made in advance and stored in the fridge for a couple of days. It is good on sausages, chops, ribs, chicken and burgers.

BURGERS:

500g lean minced steak / 1/2 large onion very finely chopped
1/2 tsp salt / Freshly ground black pepper
2 tbsp yoghurt / 1 tbsp chopped fresh parsley / Little oil for frying

METHOD

1. Mix together all the ingredients for the burgers except the oil in a large bowl.
2. Divide the mixture into 4 and shape each portion into a burger shape. Pat together lightly.
3. You can cook the burgers on a barbeque, in a preheated hot oven or in a frying pan just greased with oil. They will take 3 to 5 minutes each side but a little longer in the oven. They should still be juicy in the middle.

BARBEQUE SAUCE:

2 tbsp olive oil / 1/2 onion very finely chopped
1 clove garlic chopped finely / 2 tbsp wine vinegar
75g brown sugar / 3 tbsp soy sauce / 3 tbsp tomato ketchup
1 tsp mustard / 150ml orange or apple juice

METHOD

1. Heat the oil in a small pan.
2. Add the onion and garlic and cook without browning until soft stirring all the time. This will take about 10 minutes.
3. Add all the other ingredients and bring to the boil, stir well and cook for 10 minutes or until thick and shiny.

Salmon Parcels

SERVES 4

This recipe is great, it is very easy to prepare and serve, it can all be done in advance and there is hardly any washing up. You can feed any number of people by just increasing the ingredients. Serve with potatoes or rice.

INGREDIENTS:

4 squares of foil rubbed with a little butter or oil / 2 spring onions finely sliced / 100g carrot, peeled and cut into fine matchsticks
1 stick celery washed and finely sliced / 1 courgette washed and cut into matchsticks / 500g salmon fillet cut into 4
Freshly ground black pepper and salt / 1⁄4 tsp of dill
4 tbsp dry white wine / 4 tbsp double cream

METHOD

1. Heat the oven to 180C.
2. Bring a pan of water to the boil and plunge the vegetables into it. Cook for 1 minute and drain well.
3. Divide the vegetables into 4 and place each pile onto a piece of foil that you have bent the edges up.

4. Top each pile of vegetables with a piece of salmon.
5. Season the parcel with a little salt and pepper and sprinkle over the dill.
6. Now pour over the wine and cream and close up each parcel so that it does not leak.
7. Place on a baking tray and cook in the oven for 20 minutes.
8. Serve it in the parcel for each person to open, or on a plate out of the foil.

Scones with Cheshire Cheese and Spring Onion

SERVES 8

Scones are quick and easy to make, children love them and can make them if supervised. They are guaranteed to impress visiting aunts and grannies.

By adding different flavours you can change the basic scone mixture to savoury or sweet, but the trick with them all is to handle gently and quickly. The cheese and spring onion scones would make a great packed lunch with tomatoes, watercress and a slice of cheese or ham.

Basic scone mix

250g self raising flour / 1 tsp baking powder / 50g butter
150ml milk / little extra milk to brush the tops

For cheese and spring onion scones add

50g grated Cheshire cheese / 3 spring onions finely chopped
1/2 tsp mustard (mixed in with the milk)

OR For sweet scones add

25g caster sugar / 50g sultanas or glacé cherries

METHOD

1. Preheat an oven to 220C.
2. Sieve the flour and baking powder together into a large bowl.

3. Rub in the butter so mixture looks like breadcrumbs. Stir in any flavouring.
4. Add the milk and mix together with a knife, when just mixed turn out on to a floured surface and lightly pull together.
5. Roll out until a circle 3cm thick.
6. Either cut with a cutter to make 8 rounds or divide into eight triangles.
7. Brush with milk and put onto a baking tray.
8. Bake for about 10 minutes. They will be firm to touch and lightly brown.
9. Cool on a rack before serving.
   These freeze well but are best fresh.

Summer Berry and Pancake Gateaux with Chantilly Cream

MAKES 6 INDIVIDUAL GATEAUX

This can be made in advance and assembled at the last minute. Use whatever fruits are in season. The pancakes are of the thick drop scone variety, really easy for children to make. Use the recipe to make them for breakfast and serve with butter and jam.

Pancakes

125g self raising flour / 1/2 tsp baking powder / 25g caster sugar
1 egg / 150ml milk / 1 tsp vanilla essence / 1 tbsp sunflower oil

Filling

350g mixed berries, raspberries blackberries, strawberries and blueberries / 300ml water / 2 tbsp damson gin (optional)
75g caster sugar / 250 ml whipping cream / 1.5 tsp vanilla essence
Sprigs of mint to garnish / Icing sugar if required

METHOD

1. Mix all the pancake ingredients except for the oil together. You can use a processor or liquidiser for this. It should make a thick pouring batter.
2. Heat a little of the oil in a non-stick frying pan and put tablespoonfuls of the mixture into cook, you should aim to make 12-15 round pancakes.
3. When bubbles appear turn the pancakes over and cook until light brown.
4. Bring the water and 50g sugar to the boil.
5. Plunge the berries into this for 30 seconds and remove, save the liquid.
6. Now boil the fruit liquid frantically until it is reduced by more than half and syrupy.
7. Remove from the heat and add back in half the berries and the damson gin. Liquidize and then sieve, this makes a berry coulis.
8. Whip the cream, vanilla and 25g sugar until soft peaks.
9. Assemble to serve by putting a pancake on 6 serving plates, top with cream and berries, then another pancake and cream and berries, garnish with the mint then drizzle a little coulis around each plate to serve. Dust with icing sugar if you want.

Autumn

SEPT, OCT, NOV

Spinach and Blue Cheese Stuffed Mushrooms

Roasted Baby Beets

Spinach and Roasted Butternut Squash Risotto

Leek and Rosemary Tart

Spicy Lamb with Apricots

Pork filllet with Roasted Tomatoes and Sage

Easy Pear and Marzipan Pie

Plum Clafoutis

Seasonal Produce:

Apples, Aubergines, Beetroot, Bilberries, Blackberries, Blueberries, Brussels sprouts, Cabbage (Autumn), Celery, Damsons, Leeks, Marrows, Plums, Potatoes (Main crop), Sloes, Sweetcorn, Beetroot, Celeriac, Chestnuts, Cobnuts, Crab Apples, Fennel, Field Mushrooms, Hazelnuts, Jerusalem Artichokes, Partridge, Pheasant, Pigeon, Quinces, Rabbit, Spinach, Squash, Turnip, Venison, Watercress, Grouse, Hare, Sloes, Wild Duck.

Spinach and Blue Cheese Stuffed Mushrooms

SERVES 4 AS A STARTER OR 2 AS A MAIN COURSE

The North West produces several fine blue cheeses. Try Blacksticks Blue, Blegdale Blue or Garstang Blue and you will get a really tasty result.

INGREDIENTS:

4 large flat mushrooms / 50g chopped streaky bacon
1 small leek finely sliced / 125g baby leaf spinach
125g blue cheese crumbled / 1/4 tsp nutmeg
Freshly ground black pepper

METHOD

1. Remove the stalks from the mushrooms and place the mushroom cups into the bottom of a greased oven proof dish.
2. Fry the bacon in a large pan without any extra fat.

3. Add the leeks and chopped mushroom stalks, cook for 2 minutes until softened.
4. Stir in the spinach and cook until wilted.
5. Remove from the heat and add the cheese, season to taste with pepper and nutmeg.
6. Divide the spinach mixture between the mushrooms and cook under a medium grill for 5-8 minutes or until the cheese is bubbling and the mushrooms are cooked. Alternatively this can be cooked in a hot oven.

Roasted Baby Beets

SERVES 4

Beetroots are one of the wonder foods, full of vitamins and minerals, cheap and tasty and even better when they are small. They went out of fashion for a while unless served in vinegar but they are so much better served hot as a vegetable with roast meat.

Raw beetroot is also good grated and mixed with a little orange juice and olive oil as a salad. Remember to prepare beetroot with rubber gloves on.

You can also find golden beets occasionally which are a lovely yellow colour and a sweet flavour.

INGREDIENTS:

8 raw beetroot the size of an egg, with about 2cm of stalk left on
1tbsp olive oil / 1/2 tsp sugar / 1tsp orange juice
Seasoning to taste

METHOD

1. Preheat the oven to 180C.
2. Wash the beetroot but do not peel.
3. Place them in an ovenproof dish with all the other ingredients and cover with a lid or foil.
4. Cook in the oven for about 45 minutes or until tender, test with a skewer or knife.
5. Serve unpeeled if small or peeled if you have used larger beetroot with the juices poured over.